T0065306

I'm Possible
Not Impossible

Nelsia Sweetshiine

authorHOUSE®

AuthorHouse™ UK
1663 Liberty Drive
Bloomington, IN 47403 USA
www.authorhouse.co.uk
Phone: 0800.197.4150

Published by AuthorHouse 01/15/2016

ISBN: 978-1-5049-9728-7 (sc)
ISBN: 978-1-5049-9727-0 (hc)
ISBN: 978-1-5049-9729-4 (e)

Print information available on the last page.

Any people depicted in stock imagery provided by Thinkstock are models, and such images are being used for illustrative purposes only. Certain stock imagery © Thinkstock.

This book is printed on acid-free paper.

Because of the dynamic nature of the Internet, any web addresses or links contained in this book may have changed since publication and may no longer be valid. The views expressed in this work are solely those of the author and do not necessarily reflect the views of the publisher, and the publisher hereby disclaims any responsibility for them.

Preface

Dear Children,

It's important to know that you are special and that you are important. Therefore it is *never* okay for anybody to make you feel afraid, ashamed, fearful, or alone!

Please read on if you feel afraid, alone, useless, fearful, and ashamed. You are God's gift to the world, and you must remember that you can be a bright star, and you can be what you dream to be! If there is anybody making you feel any bad feelings, it is okay to speak up, and it is okay to speak out!

Please tell someone whom you feel you can trust. It could be your mum, dad, brother, sister, or favourite aunt or uncle. It could be your grandparents, or even your favourite teacher at school, but please tell someone.

You don't need to put up with being made to feel any of these bad feelings, or thinking that it is your fault. Because it is not! Just remember, it is never your fault, and you did nothing wrong!

There are some people who make the wrong choices and do bad things to children. These people will try to make you feel it is okay to do the things they do to you, but if something feels wrong, and you don't like what is happening to you, it is okay to say, 'No, I don't like this. No, this is wrong. No, don't touch me there. No, it hurts. No, you're not allowed to touch me there.'

If anybody makes you feel anxious, afraid, or fearful, then speak to a special person, someone whom you feel you can trust.

You are possible, not impossible!

CHILDHOOD VULNERABILITY

Chapter 1

About Me

My name is Nelsia and I am forty-six years old. I am the mother of a twenty-six-year-old son and a six-year-old daughter. I am a very straight-talking, honest person; with me, what you see is what you get. I am very much a fan of social justice, and I don't believe in pretending that bad things don't happen in life, society, and in all walks of life. In fact, brushing things under the carpet is like creating a Frankenstein monster, which is more common than we think!

I grew up with my brother and sister in a single-parent family, which is becoming the norm these days. My dad separated from my mother when my sister and I were young. The household was not a very happy household from what I can remember, especially with him there. I was a little scared and intimidated by him. Life was hard, but I was living, and that was the most important thing to me.

While growing up, we did not have the modern conveniences and the up brand name clothing, but we had the basics, for which I was grateful. We had food on the table every day night and breakfast on the table every morning. We had clean clothes on our backs and shoes on our feet. I remember being grateful for everything I received. I seemed to understand that my mother worked hard, sometimes with several jobs, and so I appreciated it – and her.

Mum was strict but fair, and I learned my morals from her. Mum did not show her feelings a lot, and she seemed to get embarrassed easily, but she showed love and kindness to her fellow human beings. She will go all out to help others. She is a very spiritual lady and had a lot of faith.

I would like to pay testimony to her and say a big thank-you. She was our mother and father, and she worked hard so that my siblings and I did not go without. My mother is still a hard-working woman, even at nearly seventy years old!

I admire her very much. She inspires me to keep striving and working hard to have what I want. Her philosophy is, 'You must work by the sweat of your brow, if you want anything good,' and I agree. By the sweat of her brow, she worked hard to make sure that we were provided for in the best possible way, and I love her! She is my Wonder Woman who runs on Energizer batteries. She never stops!

She is a wonderful, kind, humble human being who always puts others first. She is always the first to be of help to someone in need, and she does it with so much compassion and love. One thing I love about her is that she never holds a grudge, not even against her worst enemies. She's such a forgiving woman, and I learnt so much from her. I am kind of the same, because I can't hold grudges even when wronged.

The main thing to help us heal from any wrongdoing is forgiveness! Without forgiveness, we cannot move on, we cannot heal, and we will not able to move past any negative feelings or thoughts that come to us. The feelings that come out of *not* forgiving are bitterness, hate, distrust, and more emotions that can destroy you, your thoughts, your feelings, and what you are meant to grow up to be in life.

I am not preaching to anyone, but without forgiveness, you will be stuck in a never-ending negative cycle of pain, anger, bitterness, hurt, distrust of others, and taking out your pain in the form of negative words and actions on others. I have gone through these emotions myself, so I know what I'm talking about.

Forgiveness will help you to grow and be able to move past all the hurt and pain you have experienced. The first thing in helping you to heal is to speak up and speak out! Bottling up everything inside you will stifle you and cause you emotional and mental harm. Speaking up and out is the number one thing to do. I know it can be hard, because maybe you have been told to keep it a secret, or maybe threats have been made to you, but you *must* speak up and out, because it can stop this abuse from going on, and it may stop someone else from being hurt too.

You will feel such a heavy weight fall from off your shoulders and from your mind. All the burdens you may be carrying will lift. Trust me on this! A lot of people speak up and get the help they need to deal with things, but then they choose never to forgive. They continue to carry the hurt, pain, and bitterness of what they went through in their hearts.

We feel from our hearts; all our emotions come from there. It is also very good not to try to tar everybody with the same brush, or think that everyone is the same, because there are good people out there too. It is very easy to think that everyone is the same and that everyone will harm you, due to the bad things that have happened to you. It is very easy to blame everyone, and so we take things out on everyone else. We can also begin to hate ourselves, which is our way to cope and to try to forget about the bad things.

By hating ourselves and dong things to try to forget about the pain, we may start drinking, trying drugs and other things, just to ease the bad feelings. It is very easy to fall into doing these things after such trauma.

I chose to forgive straight away. Although I hurt and had all the emotions I have just spoken about, I forgave and let go of those negative emotions. I wanted to feel free after living so long with torment, and I let those emotions melt away.

What I want is the best for each and every one of you. Not only that, but I want you to recognise that you are the most important person here. Forgiveness is here to help you move on to be the person who you were placed on earth to be. Be that brilliant doctor, that studious lawyer, that caring and compassionate nurse, that dramatic actor, that angelic singer, or that wonderful writer. Do so with confidence. I don't want you to be held back because of what you went through as a child. Speak up and speak out! Get help, if you need it. Forgive and then let go!

One of the first people to forgive is yourself. After going through this kind of trauma, you may blame yourself, believing that it was all your fault. I am here to say to you that it is *not* and was *never* your fault! You never asked for it, you never wished for it, and the blame is not with you. It is with the person who should have known better. But at the same time, you must try to find it in yourself to forgive. As hard as it is, you must try. This is so you can heal and deal with what you're feeling inside.

I know it is very hard to think forgiveness, and it's easier said than done when you have been abused. I went through the temptation to hate and feel bitter about the fate I was dealt; this was mostly in my teenage years. I felt angry too. I bottled up everything, which was not good. I found it hard to speak up most times, and then other times I would force myself to try to fit in because I wanted everyone to like me. I fought my feelings and emotions on my own for a very long time before freeing myself by speaking up. I revealed what had happened to me in my early teens, and now I wish I had done so earlier. I gained an imagination from early age and daydreamed a lot. I did a lot of reading and loved writing; they became a form of escapism for me. I became maturer and wiser than my peers at school, and I became a sensitive and intuitive child, especially to others' needs. I must say that empathy has followed me into adulthood. People seem to gravitate towards me for advice, and I have a knack of soothing their fears. I think these qualities that I have gained helped me to cope well with the bad things that I experienced.

On the negative side, being abused made me become very introverted and go into myself. It was a bit like a tortoise going into his shell and not coming out until he felt safe. I lacked self-esteem and confidence in myself. Though I had friends at school, I preferred my own company a lot of the time, and I preferred to have one or two good friends rather than be part of the 'it' crowd. I preferred quality over quantity, and that trait has followed me to this day. I think that this is part of my personality. The lack of confidence sometimes spilled into anything I tried to put my hand to; I would always second-guess myself and would always be a worrier.

I would say that I still carry some of it, like the worrying, with me, but for the most part I am confident and speak up now. One would not think I was the same person back then. I used to wear a mask of happiness, but deep inside I was so sad and alone.

I understand the shame and the lack of courage that can keep you stuck and prevent you from speaking up, but in order to allow healing to start, you must speak. It is vital to your emotional and mental healing.

I love kids and hate the thought of any one of them being harmed or hurt in any way, because they are blessings from God. I am writing this book to give every child his or her voice back. If I can save even one child from going down the road of thinking that being abused sexually is their fault, then that is enough for me. My job in helping rewards my heart.

I want you to say every morning when you wake up, 'I'm possible, not impossible!' Say it several times. Say it throughout the day too. Keeping your thoughts positive brings a positive aura to you, and positive thoughts and feelings will keep your confidence growing. Trust me on that. What you give out, you get back 100 per cent.

I send out my love to all the children in the world, the next generation. They are all beautiful and bright in their own unique ways! We should be protecting each and every one of them and ensuring we lead them to be who they have been placed on this earth to be.

All the adults on the earth have that responsibility. If you are the abuser, stop right now and think about what you are turning these little human beings into. Think about what you may create. Think about their destinies, which you could be harming or changing. You are damaging their thoughts and feelings!

A lot of the time, with adults who have some sort of issue, the problem stems from childhood. Stop and think of the self-esteem and the confidence you are breaking down in these precious little beings. Please stop robbing them of their childhood innocence! Let them grow without fear or harm. They deserve to have their innocence kept intact, safe, and warm. They should be given that freedom of choice when they are able to choose, and when they are older and wiser, they can make adult decisions to allow or not to allow what happens to them.

Abusers, go get the help you need to stop! Maybe you yourself went through this trauma, and you never spoke up and got the help that you desperately needed. I am not in judgement of you, but even now, it is not too late to get the help you need. Only you can change yourself!

I know it is said that some abused people turn into the abusers, so I am not in judgement, but once again, I urge you to please do right and seek the help needed to break this cycle of harm going around and around. You need to forgive yourselves. Speak up and speak out in order to heal!

Every person has free will to choose to do good or bad, to do right or wrong, to think positively or negatively. What do you think you should choose? Will you help yourself heal?

Chapter 2

Me and That First Experience

I remember being bought into a dark room. There was no one else but me and my abuser. I used to be scared of my own shadow, afraid of being me. I used to hide behind a mask of false happiness on the pretence that I was okay, even though inside I really felt disgust, pain, and shame. I thought maybe it was my fault, and maybe I'd somehow asked for it to happen to me.

Throughout my early life, there were a few abusers, so I began to feel like maybe it was a normal thing in life. That is the biggest lie right there! Being abused as a child is not normal, not good, and not right!

I became introverted, never said much, and went into myself. I stayed in my own little world where I could feel safe. There was no one there to harm or hurt me in my own world, and it felt better for me that way.

I built a wall around my heart to try to protect myself, but I found it hard to feel good about myself. I felt lost and alone, and I wondered whether I was the only one going through hell, all on my own.

For a long time, I lived a life of shame, of feeling like I was no good. I thought I was tarnished and dirty, not good enough for anybody. Through the art of being silent, I put up with a lot from anybody who would misuse or hurt me intentionally. I got into inappropriate relationships, looking for love and acceptance from someone, anyone who would make me feel loved, special, and wanted.

I suffered from having pessimistic thoughts, and I always thought the worst of each challenge that I faced, which led me to wanting to end it all by taking my own life: Please take it from me: that is *not* the answer at all!

I wanted to write this book for all you children and young teenagers who have been going through a tough time due to painful experiences. I want to write for you, to tell you that you don't have to suffer this alone. You don't have to be afraid of feel ashamed of what you had to endure. I wrote this book to help you find your voice.

This issue can make you feel like you are in a room where you can see everything that is going on around you, but you have no tongue in your mouth to speak. The fear grips you when you're thinking, 'What will people say or think about me, if they were to find out about what happened to me? Will they treat me differently? Will they see me as a lesser person? Will they like me anymore? Will they think I am disgusting?' I became quite a fearful child. I was paranoid that if someone was not nice to me or was particularly horrible, then maybe he knew about me, and maybe I deserved not being liked. As I became older, I became distrustful of others, thinking everyone must have an agenda, especially if he or she liked me or wanted to be friends. I found it hard to believe that anyone could genuinely like me. The feelings I had inside me were like an internal battle always brewing on the inside.

I want to say that nothing is or was ever your fault! You never asked for it, and you are innocent in every way. You have nothing to feel ashamed about. You have a choice to either fight or flight, to sink or swim. That decision has to be yours and yours alone. Either you stay in prison, or you can fight for release from it. I believe you deserve to be free!

Remember, no one has the right to touch you in places that feel wrong or make you afraid and fearful. Find a person whom you feel you can trust and tell that person what has gone on, or what is still going on. There are services there to protect you and help you feel at ease with speaking. Fear not, because no one will judge you. These people are here to help you get through any difficult feelings you may have.

You may feel that if you told someone, it may break up your family at home, or it may break up relationships or friendships that you have. But please remember your safety and well-being is the most important thing, and you are number one – always! Please believe that you are not a bad person. You are a strong, bright, talented, beautiful young person who is destined to be great one day. Never let anything or anyone hold you back from being the best you can be!

Though the road has been dark, lonely, bumpy, and scary, there is a light the end of the tunnel. There is always a light at the end of it. Forgiveness, positive thinking, and letting go of the bad memories and negative thoughts are the wonderful keys to the beginning of your healing, your wellness, and a brand-new you. It's the start to your destiny and who you should be. You decide.

I chose to forgive all my abusers and to let go of all the pain, hurt, shame, fear, and bad memories. It was either they go, or my life would go into a downward spiral of negativity. I did not want negativity, so I chose to fight it.

I know that it will never change the bad things you may have suffered, but becoming bitter and full of anger, sleeping around because that's all you know, drinking alcohol, and doing drugs because you want to block out the pain – these are not answers and will not help you in the long run.

It pains my heart, because I know abused children can carry these negative traits well into adulthood, like a heavy suitcase that seems to get heavier with time, until other bad moments come along. The longer you hang onto that suitcase and carry it around, the harder it is to lighten it. I know all about the pain and anguish of carrying luggage, because I have been there too. I understand with care and concern.

I am guilty of one thing: I became a silent witness! But also remember that I let it go – and you can too! It is not too late to speak up and speak out! Speaking out will help you start to heal, as well as maybe help someone else who is going through the same thing and also needs the help and the courage to speak up. I did it, and if I could do it, so can you. Have faith and courage, and speak up and out!

Chapter 3

Fear Factor

Fear played a big part in my life, but I recognise that it was one of the last things I let go of. Fear can paralyse you and can become an unwelcome invader in all parts of your life. Fear became a part of me. It can lead you to start things and then not finish them, which some people call indecisiveness. It can lead you to second-guess yourself and your decisions. It can make you feel paranoid about things. All through my life, I felt that nobody liked me at all. Worse still, it can stop you from telling someone whom you can trust about the awful way you may be feeling.

Remember that a problem told is a problem halved. You don't have to carry this burden alone. No one can help you if you won't allow yourself to be helped. There are services to help guide and protect children and teenagers like you who have gone through a tough time and need help. The services support and, most importantly, can offer safety.

It will help to talk. Believe me, it will.

I learnt about fear and panic from an early age of five or six. The fear of what was going to happen next was what made the big, bad monster called fear grow inside me. I carried that heavy suitcase of guilt and fear around with me for the next thirteen years, until I told my mother. It was after a visit by my first abuser that I spoke up. By this time I was a young mother to a young son. My main thought was, 'I won't let my son become a victim.' In fact, my whole body screamed this out, and it all stemmed from a comment made by this person. When my mother was in the kitchen, this person said under his breath that I was good at keeping secrets! I could not believe what I was hearing, and that comment felt intimidating and made me so angry. I must admit, I saw red. I did not say anything at the time, because once again I did not want to upset my mum or anyone else at the time. I made sure when this person left, I told my mother.

Maybe this is how you feel. Maybe you don't wish to upset you mum or dad, brother or sister, grandparents, uncle, aunt, or step-parent. You may think, 'Help! What do I do?' The guilt of trying not to say anything to make sure it does not break up your family will make you feel very torn inside. The negative feelings will wrestle with your mind, like two boxers going the full rounds of their match!

The decision will whirl around in your head, making you feel confused, guilty, scared, afraid, hurt, fearful, and many other things resulting from the bad experiences.

But be brave and speak up and out. Have the courage and say to yourself, 'I am vital and important, and I'm possible. I deserve better.' In the times fear and hurt make themselves present in your life, doing so will help you on your way to being free, healing, and feeling better about yourself.

Chapter 4

My Second, Third, Fourth, Fifth, and Sixth Abuses

This chapter is about my experiences, which led to my pain, hurt, and anguish. Please don't feel sad for me, for I am not a victim anymore. I am strong, loved, and possible, not impossible!

One day I was asleep with a group of other children at the child minder's house. The room was dark because the curtains were pulled shut. I can remember being on the bed, asleep at the back of the room. I saw the door open, and a figure entered the room. I remember being led out of the room and to the kitchen. The door closed behind us, and I saw a hand signal from a male, whom I am not naming. He signalled to me to not make a sound. I was made to lie on the ground and did not know what was going to happen to me. I felt a wetness around my private area, and what I know now as oral sex was performed on me. Obviously I did not know what was going on, because I was too young to know. Now I am an adult, I do know what happened, and I'm fully aware that it was wrong!

Please, little ones, nothing is right about being touched and being encouraged or made to do something that makes you feel bad and uncomfortable. This is sexual abuse, and you need to speak up and out!

There were other instances when we were abused at the child minder's house after school. I remember I came home from school, I would be afraid to go back into the child minder's home, because I knew it could happen again. It took all my strength and courage to walk back into that flat. The fear and the panic was indescribable. I always almost wished that the child minder would be home, not just her husband. I remember this happened once, but I can't remember if it happened again. I believe I have consciously blocked this memory from my mind.

I remember sitting on the stairs one day, and even at that young age, I was pondering life and feeling sad, lonely, and alone. I also vividly remember being asked by a male stranger, who lived in the same block of flats, what was wrong and why I was sitting there on the cold steps. I remember saying, 'Nothing,' and not saying much; I also said everything was okay. The next thing I remember, this male sat beside me, put his hand in my panties, and started to touch me in my private area. I remember thinking, 'Why me? What is wrong with me? Why does this keep happening to me? I also asked myself, 'Why do I keep letting this happen to me?' I became a very withdrawn little girl, and I was very quiet and sullen. I kept everything to myself and felt alone. I did not feel normal. Internally I would cry out, 'What is wrong with me? Why am I not normal? Why is no one helping me? Why is no one protecting me?'

I felt lost and depressed all the time. My life did not seem okay; it felt like a dark place. It felt like I was the only one with a terrible secret that no one should know about it, because it was felt wrong and was shameful. I felt dirty, ashamed, and even guilty. School was the only place I could get a little bit of relief. I felt safe when at school, where I could play with my friends and forget about things for a few hours. But even then, I did not have many friends because I had built a barrier around me. I found it hard to relate to other children and was unable to let them get close. I walked around like a child who had the whole world on her shoulders. Every day felt like a nightmare, because I had to return to that child minder and wait for my mother to collect me and my sister. I found out this child minder's husband abused another young female child on that same block, and for a while, I carried that guilt around with me for years. I blamed myself that if I spoke up and out, it might not have happened to her too.

As for the stranger who abused me on the stairs, I don't recall seeing him again, so I don't know whether he was just visiting a friend who lived there, or whether he actually lived there himself.

The next abuse, was by a relative. The relative was older and should have known better. I remember my sister and I going with a few of my relatives to play in one of their bedrooms, where we huddled on top of a bed. Lots of legs and arms went everywhere. Eventually I felt a hand and fingers reaching into my panties. It was a state of confusion in my mind, where time once again felt like it stood still. I remember wondering, when this was going to end. Why was I subjected to abuse? Was I the one who made these things happen? I wondered what was in me that made these things keep happening to me.

Much of my younger life was confusion and emotional trauma. As I got older, I began to feel dirty and useless, like I did not belong in the world. I thought that because these things kept happening to me, it meant I was no good. I felt misunderstood. These abuses made a validation in my mind that I deserved it, and that I should just put up with it because that was my life. I grew up a very scared and confused girl. I felt like no one understood me, and no one cared. Life did not feel fair to me. I hated my life.

I used to look at other children and young people, and I'd think how lucky they were to be them. They did not have to feel afraid. They were lucky to not be me. I hated being me. I hated what I looked like, and that also led to a very big dislike of having my picture taken. I hated my looks. I hated everything about me. I felt like I was the unluckiest girl in the world and that nothing would ever get better. I carried that feeling around for many years. It is a very big, heavy burden to carry when one is so young.

There was another instance of being abused by another man when my mother went abroad. I remember being asked to sit on a sofa in a house, and I did so partly because I was afraid and partly because I was in someone else's home and did not want to be disrespectful. I remember being told that I was pretty, and he asked if I had a boyfriend. I remember my legs being stroked. Even when every fibre in my body cried out that something was odd about this situation, I did not feel strong enough to speak out or say no. I then remembered being asked to go lie on the bed in the bedroom, which was opposite the living room. I remember getting that sick feeling in my stomach that it was all happening again. But what could I do? I was just a young child of eleven, and I wondered how could I fight or get away from a grown man. I did as I was asked.

This man first asked me if I was a virgin. I did not even know what being a virgin meant. He kissed me and touched my private parts. He made me touch his private parts too, which I did not want to do. I felt repulsed with him and with myself. I felt lost and dirty, and I thought this was all my life was going to be, and I would never get out of this ongoing nightmare!

There was another event where I allowed myself to be touched as a thirteen-year-old, because I thought that was all my life was about. Why was I to believe anything else when, all through my young, tender life, this was all that happened? I became very hard on myself and hated myself. I did not value myself as a young child should. I had regular thoughts of ending my life. I thought long and hard about it, and I believed that suicide was my only way out of this nightmare.

I eventually took a load of tablets one day, when I could not take anymore of life. But something in me snapped, and it was like a light bulb came on. and I ended up calling the emergency services, who sent an ambulance to rescue me. I really did not want to die. I did not want to leave behind my mother and family. I did not want to leave behind pain and hurt. I just couldn't do it. Even though I could not go through with ending my life, it did not stop me from having persistent thoughts about it. My self-esteem was shattered. The abuse felt like a never-ending, vicious cycle that would haunt me for the rest of my life.

I want to say to young people that even though I went through these horrible events, I am here to stay.

I remember being asked why I had done what I done. I did not tell them the real reason. The shame of people knowing was too much to handle. All I knew at that time was my suicide attempt was a cry for help! It was a cry for someone to save me. It was a cry for validation that I was normal and was a good person.

I had to write these things down, because some of you may have gone through things like this. It may have been painful to read what I have written, but I have done it so that you can see although I went through these things, even though I suffered anguish and torment, I am alive and well. I got over the hurt and pain, and most important to me, I got over all the shame!

I want to say that I have gotten over what I believe has been a very hard battle for my life. I stood up time and time again after being knocked down. After every abuse that I have been through, every single time, I have gotten stronger, and I recognise that I am a winner. I am strong. I do deserve to live in harmony and peace, in a life full of love and abundance, just like anyone else. I learnt to love myself and love everyone. I learnt to forgive myself and to forgive my abusers As I have done this, so can you! I know that I am possible, not impossible, and that there is nothing that I cannot be or do!

Forgiveness is one of my strengths. People are amazed at how large my capacity is to show forgiveness towards others, even when they have wronged me. I do not have it in me to be hurtful, hateful, or horrible to others. I always tend to take people at face value, and I tend to believe that everyone is good. I don't think we are perfect human beings, but I do think that we sometimes make bad decisions. It is good to forgive. As I said earlier, without it, we who have been through events and traumas like this will find it hard to heal completely. Just forgive and then forget. Although we know that these things happened, and we can never change the fact that they did, we can choose to forget them. Think of it as putting that memory into a box and burying it, because that memory is dead, and we do not need it anymore. It is not alive and cannot harm you anymore. Forgive the abuser, build a bridge, and walk over it, never to look back. It is a brand-new day and a new you.

I want you to see that you can be whatever you put your mind to be. You can do whatever you wish to do when you grow up. By this I mean whatever job you want, and whatever you aspire to do. I am saying that you did nothing wrong. You are relevant, you are great, and you are wonderful. You're lovely, sweet, and strong, and you can be full of confidence! Ending your life is not the way out of this. That will only hurt the people you love and who really love and care for you.

Think of how devastated your family and those whom truly love you will feel, if you take the easy way out. They will feel hurt and think it is their fault. They want to see a beautiful person grow up, and they want to see you blossom into the bright star that you are and should be! I want to encourage you to look up, be bold, and stay strong.

Please, please speak up and speak out. You can get over any pain or hurt that you have gone through. If you are going through it now, speak up! It will only stop if you do.

Nelsia Sweetshiine

You are possible, not impossible!

I love you and want to see you be the biggest, brightest star that you deserve to be! No one and nothing should stop you. If I can do it, I know you can do it too. I believe in you, but you have to believe in yourself as well!

Chapter 5

Bright Skies, Bright Sun, Bright Life

Simply releasing your hurts, pains, and fears will be very invigorating. The way forward is looming large, and you will begin to feel like nothing can harm you ever again. It will feel like every time an obstacle comes in your way, you will find the strength that is inside you. You are stronger than you think! Believing that is another key to being the great person you actually are. No one can stand in your way but you!

Think of it this way. You need food to keep alive to be strong, and you need petrol to enable a car to move, right? In order for your life to become alive, be strong, and move forward, you have to get out of your way. Stop with the anger, with the bitterness, with the fear, with every bit of negative thinking. You need to know that you are strong and confident – and that you must believe it. It is vital that you believe that you are all these things.

The last vital thing is that you must believe you deserve good things. Absolutely! Just like anyone else, you deserve love, happiness, success, wealth, joy – every good thing that there is to be had!

I believe that no matter who we all are, there is no one better than anyone else; we are all equal because we are all human beings, and each of us deserves respect, love, care, warmth, and joy. Though there may be some in this world who have lots of money, none of it makes them better than you or me. Whatever we gain on earth, when we die, we cannot take it with us. Whether you're a child, teenager, adult, or older person, each and every one of us should be respected in every way. Our bodies, minds, and thoughts should be given that respect.

One other important thing is that although I have been through hard times in my life, I am still kind, loving, and forgiving to all. This is a very important key. It could have been easy to hate everyone and the whole world, but that was not going to help me heal. I say, let it all go. It *will* help you to heal, I promise you. Positive thinking breeds positive energy, and what you put out returns back to you as positive energy, bringing along with it positive events and a positive abundance of confidence and renewed self-esteem. After a while, you won't recognise the hurting and negative person you felt like previously.

You may not even see what I am saying to you yet. I promise if you take each day one at a time, making small steps, you will suddenly see what I have been trying to say. Slowly but surely, you will!

This life is a journey, so why not make it an awesome journey? You will not know how far you can go until you have the courage to do it, and if at first you fall down, get right back up and try again. You are much stronger than you think! Believing it is a key to being the great person that you can be. No one can stand in your way but you!

Chapter 6

Grey Days, Black Nights

There will be times where you will feel like the whole world is against you, and you feel unloved and unwanted. You may feel ashamed and afraid that if anyone knew about what you have been through, you would be ridiculed, be made fun of, and not believed. Perhaps you suffer from the feeling of disgust with yourself, or feeling hopeless in life. But you need to realise and believe that you did nothing wrong at all.

If there is one thing, I want to get across, it is it's not your fault – you did nothing wrong!

I am writing this to you who have been through terrible abuses and things that your innocent eyes never should have seen, and I am telling you that there can and will be better days ahead for you. Eventually you will only see bright blue skies and nothing but the hope of better things to come.

You were and may even still be a victim at this very moment, but you do not need to stay one. Dare to speak up and out. There will always be a person you can trust, and that will be another key to your freedom from fear, pain, and the hurt you feel.

Every person was given the special gift of free will, which means that you have another special tool, another special key to freedom from your pain, fears, hurt, and possibly the anger or hate you feel towards the person who made you feel all these negative feelings. These feelings can end up harming you and can lead you into doing, saying, and bringing negative things and situations into your life!

I am telling you this because I want the best for you. I want you to have the best possible start in the wonderful life you could have, if you don't let these negative thoughts and feelings enter your head, mind, and heart.

I talk from experience of what I have been through, and though I recognise that not everyone's path will be the same, I know how I let negative thoughts and feelings harm my way forward in life.

The first thing you have to do, little ones, is forgive yourself for thinking that you made these things happen to you, or that it was your fault. You then have to try to forgive the person who did these things. Although it is easier said than done, it is something that will help you feel better and start your inner healing.

You also need to remember that bad things will happen in life, and you cannot always control why or how they will happen. However, you must look deep inside yourself and be strong.

I know that you can be strong. Children are resilient little things. Some are stronger in personality than others, but you are all strong in your own ways. Every one of us has strength inside, and if we search for it, it will find us!

Every day when you awake, say these words to yourself.

- I am not to blame.
- I am not a victim and never will be.
- Nothing can harm or hurt me again.
- I am a good boy/girl.
- I am worthy of love.
- I am strong and full of confidence.
- I deserve respect.
- I deserve kindness.
- I have people who really love me, and I love them.
- I am the best and will be the best at what I put my mind to do.
- I am strong.
- I am emotionally strong.
- I am full of confidence.

- I will be a source of encouragement to those who hurt inside.
- I will not be hateful.
- I will not be selfish towards others.

Saying some of these things to yourself will help you feel better. It may not happen overnight, but you will start to feel stronger within yourself, day by day.

Sometimes pain can lead to people doing or getting into all kinds of bad trouble, like drinking too much alcohol, taking illegal drugs, harming themselves, and feeling like they want to end their lives. Maybe they start to look for love in all the wrong places, with people whom they would not normally be with. But these things help you recognise the tools that can hurt you. We tend to look for something that will numb or block the pain and hurt that we are feeling, or we get involved in these things so we can mask the hurt, guilt, and shame.

If you ever get to this point, then you can see your doctor or seek specialist help. Not everyone will have to see a doctor or specialist. I did not go to see one, but everyone is different. It depends on your personality; some people are stronger than others. Some sensitive people may not cope as well. I myself was a sensitive child who took everything to heart, and I took things personally too, but at the same time I developed this inner strength, and I kept getting up and fighting. It is this same strength that made me feel I could overcome the feeling of guilt and shame. I said to myself, 'I can do this. I am not a victim, never was, and never will be.' I feel that if I can do it, so can you! I really do believe you can do it, if you put your mind to it.

Sometimes it is not even the physical things that happen to you that scar you; but the emotional thinking and the thoughts in your mind afterwards that create the damage. Before doing all the things above that I have suggested can help you, first you have to speak out and tell somebody whom you can trust! This will be the first and best key to use. Do not bottle things up for years, like I did. Doing so made me painfully shy and afraid to speak up. It became a burden, like a heavy, dark, guilty secret, and I was the only one who knew about it. I felt like I had to carry the whole weight of the world on my shoulders, alone! I built a wall around myself and my heart to try to protect myself from further harm. I did not feel understood by anyone. I always felt misunderstood, like I was useless and was good for nothing. I began to look for love in all the wrong places with people who only wanted what they could get; they never really cared about me. This happened because I wanted to feel loved and wanted. I did not value myself at that time, but I do now.

I write to little ones out of love for you all! You don't need to hang onto past hurts and negative feelings, like I did. You are valuable, vital, and precious. You are someone great, and you should be full of life with purpose. Let go, live, and be who you were meant to be!

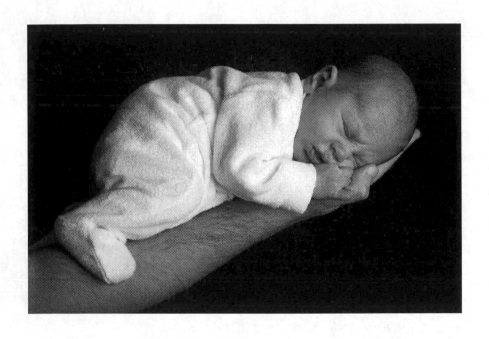

Chapter 7

Our Duty of Care to the Kids

We adults need to help our children by speaking to them, listening to them, and educating them. We should warn them of the potential threats that they could face in life.

Anyone can hurt and feel pain throughout life, but as long as we don't hang on to 'I am a victim' thoughts, we can overcome anything! I am living proof that we can. I suffered it many times at the hands of different people, but I survived. You can survive and get better too.

Most abuse happens with one person over a period of time, but obviously in my case, it went beyond that. I grew up thinking that everything that happened was part of growing up, part of childhood; that was just how it was. I thought that every child went through that.

I would always get asked 'Why are you so sad?' or 'Why do you walk with your head down?' or 'Cheer up, it may never happen!' I used to get told that there was a sadness behind my eyes. I wasn't going to tell them why that sadness was there, but they were right.

Because of what I what I went through, I led a confused scared existence. I felt unloved and alone in my pain, hurt, and fears. I went into myself a lot and became introverted. I used to dream about how my life should be and how perfect it would be to find my happy ever after. It was only when I became older and saw things for myself – like news of missing children or abused children in the media – that I became enlightened. What I had gone through was not normal and certainly was not right. To see the weeping family members so upset and grieving reduced me to tears. Even now, I get upset – and yes, a little angry – when I see any story relating to children being harmed in any way.

I am a very sensitive person, and I suppose that the one thing that I can take as a positive about my personality and my experiences is that I am very sensitive to others and their needs. That goes for anyone, not just children. I care about people's needs, and I do tend to burn myself out trying to be there for others who are going through a hard time. A lot of the time, I leave my own needs on the back burner. If there is anything that I can do to help, whether it be giving advice, time, or money if I have it, then I am there. That has always been my ways, and it will never change.

The enormity hit me when I was suddenly faced with the truth of my early life. I began to say to myself, 'If I have any children myself, I will do anything in my power to protect them from what I went through.' That's why I felt so strongly that I needed to write this book: I want to protect not just my children but all of them. If there is even one child or teenager whom I can help with my words, then it would make me so very happy and proud to have been a part of the healing process, no matter how small. It would give me great personal satisfaction.

I believe that no child should ever have to go through this trauma, but if she ever does go through it, I want to try to be a voice for her.

I truly believe that this trauma can change someone's destiny in life; it can alter thought patterns and can damage one's confidence and self-esteem, which can follow a person all the way into adulthood. People who are abused can struggle to know who they are, what they want to be, and where they want to go in life. It can stunt or stop that natural growth that should happen in their lives and divert them onto a different path. I have seen so many people with addictions to drink, drugs, sex, and self-harming, as well as suicidal thoughts. I have to be honest: when I see adults who are addicted to drugs, alcohol, or prostitution, it saddens me. I never judge, because I don't know what happened in that person's life for him to end up in that position. I am not saying that every one of those people was abused, but I know that most are running away from the realities of life, and some are trying to blank out painful memories they want to forget.

I work in an environment where I come across these people all the time. When speaking to some of them, what strikes me is that there was a common theme running through their lives. There was some kind of trauma or abuse that they grew up with from childhood, and they tried to run away from it or block it out. Let's face it: to some of these people, when they are drunk or high, they don't have to remember those bad memories, those nightmares that they had to live through. But what saddens me is that some of these addictions are killing them, and it is painful to see.

I do believe that one of the reasons they are going through these things is they never dealt with the pain and anxiety way back then. Their way to cope is to get drunk and take drugs so they can forget. I feel their pain in my heart.

They are obviously in pain, because I know where they are coming from and understand.

Most people get to this point because they are trying to forget some sort of trauma that happened to them. This new abuse may be the only way that they see as being able to cope. Also, some can also be affected by what they saw happening to someone else (a loved one or a friend), but they felt helpless or powerless to do anything. The guilt takes hold of them and their thoughts.

I believe that children are our future, and they have the right to be able to grow as children in safety. They should not have their childhoods stolen from them. They have the right to keep their childhoods intact! They have the right to say, 'No, it is not okay to touch me at all.'

I recognise that some abusers may have been abused themselves, or they suffered some kind of trauma in their own lives, but I will not make excuses for anyone. Every man and woman has a conscience and knows right from wrong. People are given free will to choose whether to do what they know is right.

Why destroy another human being's life? Why destroy a child's innocence, especially when you know the pain and suffering it could cause? And why, if you have been through it yourself and know what you went through, would you do it to another? Why inflict a life-changing misery on a child, possibly changing that child's destiny forever?

Parents have a duty to sit their children down and advise them of the bad things that could come up in life. The rose-coloured glasses need to come off. There also needs to be active monitoring of what your children watch. This also applies to schools and any establishment dealing with children. I believe it should start young, because their little brains are sponges, and they take in everything. I do know that some people would not want to have that talk at such tender years, but we are living in a world that has changed a lot, and with the rise of the media, smart phones, and the Internet, a lot of these young children have access and see things that they should not be subjected to. There are dangers lurking around every corner. We need to stay vigilant to protect the next generation.

I believe that not only educational subjects should be taught in school. The subject of safety should be incorporated into the curriculum too. Just the other day, I saw a news report about teenagers and young children sending graphic images to each other and to someone whom they think is the same age as them, when in fact the person was not who they thought! We are living in serious times, and this is a serious topic; it should not be swept under the carpet.

Sexual abuse is happening all over the world and in all societies, from the rich to the poor. In fact, there are some groups that think it is okay to sleep with children! There is something very wrong here! Now, I am not bashing parents, because I am one, so I do know how hard it can be in this fast-paced world. But something needs to be done to protect our children. Some may think that it is drastic and that young children should be left to just be children, and to some extent I agree, but I feel so passionately about this subject that I believe that they need to be made a little more aware. Kids, especially the younger ones, have an innocent naiveté that can be exploited, especially with the abusers grooming the children and use the art of gaining trust at the beginning.

Children are soaking up information all the time, and if enough information gets soaked early, children will feel better informed about what to do if they ever find themselves in such a situation. They would be able to deal with the aftermath of the negative feelings and thoughts that can overwhelm them later on. I say forewarned is forearmed!

I want to say once again to every child or teenager reading this book: know that none of it was or is your fault. You did nothing wrong!

While growing up, I felt I had no voice. I grew up with a level of maturity higher than all my friends at school. I was the serious one in the group. People always saw me as a serious person. As I said previously, I became terribly shy and introverted. I had nightmares of monsters coming into my bedroom at night to get me. I used to sleep with my head under the covers. I wet my bed until I was about ten. I found that I could never look anyone in the eye, and when I walked anywhere, it was with my face downwards. I did not like myself much. That was no way to live life. I suffered with low self-esteem and never believed I could do anything right. I always saw myself as a failure. This all stemmed back to the sexual abuse, which robbed me of my life for a long, long time. This type of situation happens all around us in every walk of life, in every society, class, race, creed, and background. It is something that I believe is often swept under the carpet, never to be talked about.

As ashamed as I am to say this, there are some people who know where there is abuse going on right now, but they close their eyes, minds, ears, and hearts to it! Some of these people are influential people who refuse to talk about it, because to them, not talking about it is a way of saying it is not happening.

I think it is fair to say that given recent media on this subject, it is going on, and it will continue to go on. A lot of influential people know the truth. The abuser and his victim and God all know the truth, and when we think we have gotten away with things, karma has a very good way of dealing with us. Nothing hidden stays hidden – it is always revealed!

We are living in a culture where nothing matters but oneself. 'So long as me, myself, and I are okay, then what does it matter what happens to anyone else?' It is a selfish way to live, but that is what I see going on.

We all have a duty of care towards the next generation, and we don't want a broken or damaged one. Every adult has a duty of care to the little ones.

I am here to say abuse is not right, and every human being who is alive and breathing on earth right now has a right to not be abused. Our duty of care is to protect the children. We must stop and destroy the evil of negative emotions, pain and hurt, and all the baggage that will become attached to these little ones. That baggage could change their way of thinking, behaving, and interacting in such a way that the lights in their little souls are dimmed or put out!

We need to stop this abuse before the horse has bolted out of the stable. In other words, we must stop it before it starts. We can't wait and then say, 'If only I had known.' We need to be vigilant now, not when it is too late!

Chapter 8

Time Is Truly a Healer

One of the greatest healers of the past is time. Healing takes time, and people will be at different stages in their healing because we are all different, with different personalities. Some are stronger than others, and some are weaker, but with time, the healing comes. Memories become more distant, and the pain and hurt become less painful, though not forgotten. Time takes away that unhealthy grip it has on the abused.

My aim is to highlight that children are unable to understand or process what is happening to them, especially if they're very young. The enormity of it can be very overwhelming. Like me, some may grow up believing that this is normal, especially if it is something that is happening to them on a regular basis. It happened so many times through my formative years that I felt it was normal, and I thought that every child had to go through it. I did not understand that it was wrong. But I will say that it made me feel different than everyone else. A deep sadness overtook my soul and spirit, and I felt set apart from everyone else. That is when a deep sense of shame came into play.

As I grew up, at school they used to show the Stranger Danger videos, like, 'Say no to strangers,' or the 'Charley says, "Don't talk to strangers"' adverts. When I saw these videos, I became more and more aware that it was wrong. For me the shame got worse, because I now knew that it was wrong, and I wondered why or how I'd allowed it to happen without telling someone about it. I felt it was part of my secret. It was like something was telling me that it was wrong. I became afraid of what other kids felt about me, and in my teens, I used to wonder what others' opinions of me were. I cared what they thought about me, and I have to say, this feeling followed me into my mid-twenties. It was not until my late twenties that I found peace with myself through finding faith.

I am not saying that everyone should go find a church, but it helped me a lot at that time. I became self-assured, and I did not care about anyone's opinion about me. I gained self-confidence, and my self-esteem skyrocketed. I finally became my own person, with views and opinions that I was not afraid to say. I had found my voice! I gained my own mind and could rely on my own feelings with conviction. My inner strength became so strong that when bad things happened, I would not crumble; I seemed to gain an inner strength that took over.

When bad things happen, it can overwhelm a person at the time, but I always picked myself up, dusted off myself, and kept moving. I got back into that boxing room and restarted the fight. I always said to myself, 'This problem's not going to win. I will win.' I became stronger in mind and feelings. I felt invincible and powerful, and I felt that nothing could harm me or bring me down. I wouldn't allow it to beat me! I began to love myself for who I was, and I began to value myself. I did not look for love in wrong places anymore.

I felt ugly growing up, and I couldn't even have a picture taken. I hated pictures of myself. I totally love pictures now and feel attractive. I am what you call a selfie junkie!

My point is that you can get over the pain and hurt; it does not need to go on for a lifetime. It will be a one step at a time, in a 'one day at a time' healing process. Nothing can be rushed, but I promise that you can and will heal.

Chapter 9

Kids, not everyone who gives gifts is genuine. Keep your eyes and ears open, and always follow your gut instincts. Your instincts are never wrong!

Please remember and understand that although it is very nice to receive gifts and goodies, but if someone keeps giving you gifts or keeps trying to get you to do things that you don't feel comfortable with, then that is a red flag that should be telling you to stop. Do not take any gifts or presents from that person, and do not do anything that he or she asks you to do, especially if it does not feel right to you. Please tell someone straight away, someone whom you feel you can trust, about what has happened.

If you are getting a gut feeling that something is wrong, that is your intuition inside you trying to warn you that you should stay away from this person and not take the gifts, presents, or money. This person is trying to gain your trust by giving you these gifts and nice things, which makes him or her look ok to you. If you get asked for special favours in return, these may be danger signs. Please heed them and mention it to someone you trust, especially if you feel confused or scared. This person wants you to feel like you can trust him or her, and that because he or she gave you these gifts, it is okay to do bad things to you. He or she knows that if you accept the gifts, then you will find it hard to say no to them and what they may want you to do. They know that you will feel guilty about taking the gifts, and that you will feel like you owe them for having given you these things.

If you say no, they will try to make you feel bad or guilty by saying things like, 'Don't you trust me? I am a good person. I gave you all those nice things.' They may even make threats or get angry, when they see that you are very aware about what they are trying to trick you into doing.

If this sort of thing happens to you, I advise you to tell someone, and warn your friends about how to keep safe and what to do and say. Pass it on in order to help another child or young person. To you teens, this person may even try to entice you into drinking alcohol, or he may promise you cigarettes or something that you have been wanting to try because you think it is cool. Please stop and think to yourself, 'Why is this person doing this? What is his motive?' If you are not sure, please tell someone what has happened.

Everyone has the ability to feel fear. Take a mouse, for instance. If you try to corner one, it gets afraid and scampers away, or it tries to find a way past you and away from what it thinks is danger. Mice may be small, but they are clever little things. Instead of heading towards the danger, they run away as fast as their legs can carry them.

Please, please talk up. Try to dig deep and find the courage that I know is inside you. Once again, if someone has made you feel uncomfortable, scared, afraid, tearful, or guilty, or someone has tried to make you do something you do not want to do, speak up and out! It could save your life in more ways than one, and it could also help another child or young person.

I am telling you all these things to help keep you safe. Be aware so that you do not fall into the trap of any potential abusers.

If anyone tries to give you gifts and presents, and then asks you to do this or that with him, please tell someone whom you trust straight away. If something or someone makes you feel afraid, you need to tell someone straight away. Please speak up and out!

Chapter 10

Free, but Still Feel Like a Prisoner

There will be times where you have come through the worst of the physical side and pain of the actual abuse, but mentally and emotionally it can leave deep wounds and scars of hurt. You will feel emotions like fear, anger, and betrayal, and sometimes these feelings will linger for a long time, well after the abuse has taken place. These are the feelings than can come back to haunt you time and time again. It can feel like a broken record that will not stop.

I felt like a bird trapped in a cage who desperately wanted to be free. In fact if I could be any animal, it would be a bird. Back then I felt like a sparrow, but now it would definitely be an eagle, such a strong, majestic bird that can bring down its prey with focus and precision. It is a solitary bird that flies alone. The only time it will fly with another is with its mate. It's odd that you never see eagles flying in a group. In fact, the eagle is always flying high. Then it will perch on a rock and sharpen its beak, which it can then use to pluck out weak feathers that slow down its flight in the sky. The eagle can then soar high again in the sky.

The eagle is just like us. When we are feeling down and depressed, we retreat into ourselves, not desiring to be social and just wanting to be alone. Sometimes in that alone time, we can gather our thoughts and think clearly. After this we can begin to heal and become stronger, and soon we'll soar just like that eagle. Those weak feathers of the eagle slow it down and create obstacles in the way it was made to fly. Once it has taken the alone time to clear out the weakened feathers, it can continue being who it should be. Sometimes bad things will happen to slow us down in life, but only by doing something can we move on. I like the fact that once the eagle is focused on where it is going, it will never let anything stop it from getting to its destination. The eagle will not let anything like a few weak feathers get in its way to where it knows it needs to be. The eagle is a determined bird, full of confidence and vigour.

The reason I bring up the eagle is that sometimes in life, we have to get rid of the negative thoughts and feelings that can slow down our flights through life. Just like that eagle, who knows which weak feathers to pluck out, we need to do the same by getting rid of the negative so that the positive can come in. Let go. It is harder done than said, but with a little bit of courage and confidence, you can do it!

If we think negatively, all we are going to bring back to us is more negative thoughts. Think of it like this. When you're really hungry, you want to eat lots. Once you think a negative thought, you begin to feed that thought, and because of the other little fears you might have, more and more negative thoughts come in. Then by the time you know it, you are feeling full of fear and doubt, which can make you feel low, depressed, and down. Please try to think positive things; surround yourself with positive people and positive activities. If you start to think positively, you will feel more positive, which will present you with even more positive thoughts and feelings. It is important to surround yourself with them. Negative brings negative, and positive brings positive.

Chapter 11

One of My Wishes

As a child, I used to wish that I was a bird. I used to daydream most days about being one. There would be days that I would take myself to the park across the road and sit for hours, looking into the sky and watching the birds fly around. I also loved to watch all animals, and I'd think to myself that they were lucky because they were free and walked around with no cares or worries. The freedom birds represented in my mind was my escape route. I felt like a prisoner in my mind, as if I was in a cage with bars around me all the time.

I suppose that's how most of you may feel. Maybe you are paralysed with fear and doubts, and you can't move on from the things you've been through and seen. But I am here to tell you that you don't have to live in a cage, because there is a key to your release. There is a big key waiting for you to pick it up and use it. It all starts inside you. The key is there, if you look clearly enough!

Reach out to someone with whom you feel safe. Open your mouth and speak. The first step to healing and to your freedom from pain is to tell someone. It could be one of your family members, your favourite teacher, your best friend, or anyone that makes you feel safe. I know it is easier said than done, but trust me when I say it is the only way to flying as high and as free as a bird.

If you look at a bird, see how it flies without a care in the world, carelessly gliding through the air in the blue skies. It is secure in the knowledge that it's in control of its life, with no one telling it when to stop and come down until it wants to.

Just as that bird has all the control when he flies, you can too! Only you can control your thoughts and actions. If you want to feel positive, you have to think positively and do positive things. Do good things that you know are good for you and in your best interests. No one can do this but you.

It's your time to get up. Stand up with that little bit of faith and strength you have left in you, and take back your life into your hands. Demand your life back! Say right now, 'You did not win! You will never win. You have not and will never destroy me, my spirit, my will, who I am, and who I will be!'

You are stronger than you will ever know. Every single human being has free will to choose to do good or to do bad. Unfortunately, some people choose to do things that they know are wrong. But please don't think that everyone is like this. That's the big lie you could begin to believe, especially when it seems like everything in your life is not working out like it should. When everyone you come into contact with doesn't act in the best way, it is so easy to think life won't ever get better. But I tell you that the more you think negatively, the more you'll attract negative things, events, and people towards you. Positive thoughts and actions are another key to your freedom through life. I guarantee this!

You are important and vital, and no one can stop your progress from moving on from the pain and abuse you have gone through, EVEN if you are going through something now. You can be that free bird! Be as free as you can be. Only you can stop yourself; only you can get in the way of you.

Look at the bigger picture and visualise what or where you would like to be in the future. Then strive to go forward. Each and every time you fall down, through whatever setback may come, simply get right back up and keep going until you get to your desired destination.

Always raise the bar higher. If you fall down, get back up and try even harder. Don't give up. Never be satisfied with where you are when you fall. If you're not at the place you want to be, keep moving until you get there.

Some of the people you see, like the people in the media who are at the top of their professions, come from all walks of life and have gone through many ups and downs. Some have probably gone through what you and I have gone through. But they never let their bad experiences stop them from getting to the top. They never let it paralyse them from moving forward. They never let it become an excuse to not try.

There is a saying I liked from the very first time I heard it: 'Build a bridge and walk over it.' It means that although things happen, we can make the choice to get up and keep moving forward, without looking back.

Today, I am grateful that I am alive. Many people are not grateful to have life. I am grateful for the good and the bad things that have happened to me, because however unfortunate the bad was, it gave me experience and taught me lessons. The bad taught me what to do and what not to do. It taught me how and when to speak, and when not to speak. It has taught me compassion, love, patience, and kindness. It has given me what I call a superhuman strength inside. It has taught me right from wrong on many levels. It has taught me to never do unto others what I would not want done to myself. I have this inner strength, and no matter what bad experiences I have gone through, I am an overcomer. When I fall down, I keep getting back up and continuing the fight. I have this mindset that I must win and that nothing can beat me.

Go on. Be that bird that I know you can be!

Chapter 12

Learn to Live for You in the Now, Not the Past

When we go through trauma, it can cloud our whole lives for the worse. The course of being the type of people we were meant to be can be changed. Trauma can affect us in all sorts of ways that we cannot see at first.

I grew up with low self-esteem and was painfully shy because of my trauma. The effect of the abuse and the trauma it caused had a huge impact on who I became. Some of us go through these things and bury the trauma deep into the backs of our minds, because we want to forget. However, that means that we are not dealing with the root problems.

Lack of self-esteem can cause you to second-guess yourself and your decision making. You can end up living your life in confusion and not knowing which way to turn. Sometimes trauma can make you try to please everyone, because you want the love and attention that you did not feel when you were younger. You try to compensate by trying to live your life to suit everyone else's needs and wants. Then you end up doing everything that everyone else wants you to do, but you end up doing everything to please others, as opposed to pleasing yourself.

Resentment can build up as you realise that you are not doing anything for yourself and are simply existing to please others. Do what you feel in your heart will please you. Yes, it is good to help others and please them, but what are you doing for *you*? You are number one.

In fact, because of the trauma and the feeling that you have no self-esteem, you do not feel any self-worth, and so you may not even love or like yourself, which leads you to help everyone else without consideration for your own wants or needs. This can be very exhausting mentally and emotionally. You have started to put everyone else's needs and wants above your own desires for your life. You may even have dreams, aspirations, goals, and milestones that you should have reached by now, but you have pushed them back time and time again for others. Time stands still for no one, so by the time you look, your whole life may have passed you by, and you have not accomplished all that you should have because you wanted to please others. Please don't be a martyr and throw your life away. Live your life in the here and now – and most important, for you!

Love yourself. If you don't love yourself, how can you love anyone else? You dear ones are the most important. Take the time to heal your hearts and minds. Love yourselves, your warts and all. No one is perfect, because there is no such thing as perfect. True love is accepting others as they are, not as how you want them to be.

Unconditional love is the love in which I believe. I went through the mill of life, but I unconditionally love myself now. Therefore I can unconditionally love others.

Nothing is perfect, and nothing lasts forever. We are only on earth for a short while. Healing starts with you, and it starts in your heart with forgiveness to yourself and to others regarding all the horrible things that you may have endured. Hanging onto bitterness can hurt you as a human being, and it can cause distress to everything around you. Forgive and let go. Where there was darkness, there will be light; where there was no laughter, there will be joy; where there was no love, there will be love.

I love you all. Live for yourself in the now, not the past.

Chapter 13

Message to the Adults

This is not a subject, anyone likes to think about, let alone discuss, but it is a huge dilemma going on all around the world. It is happening, even as we speak. As I said before, we adults need to be vigilant about signs that we may see. If something does not feel right about what we are seeing, we need to act on our gut instincts.

Many children being abused may not know how to tell someone that they are being abused, because they feel a huge amount of guilt and shame. I know that I had these feelings, and it was not easy to carry them around. They felt like a big burden encasing my whole life.

Please remember that children who have been or are being sexually abused will more than likely be scared into not talking. They're made to feel that if they talk, something bad will happen to them or their family members. They do not understand that they are being manipulated by their abusers. They will be made to feel that the abuse is their fault. I know that the guilt and shame of being abused can reduce the chances of children ever talking about it.

Some people will block out this part of their lives as if it did not exist; this helps them to feel that they are normal, just like everybody else. They get a false sense of security by pretending that it did not happen at all.

If you ask some people who have been abused about their childhoods, it is likely they don't remember parts of it. We have a duty of care to protect children, because if abuse is not discovered, the damage to the children can last well into adulthood, and perhaps a lifetime. If they do not receive the right kind of help or support, it can be very damaging to them, and it can also be very upsetting for their loved ones.

The effects of sexual abuse can create a lifetime of negative consequences for the abused. It can lead to depression, eating disorders, and the inability to cope with their emotions, stressful situations, and life in general. They can also suffer anxiety, emotional issues, sadness, low self-esteem, and anger towards society.

If you notice your child or adolescent is acting in a manner that does not feel right, try to speak to the child; get her to open up to you and relieve her pain. She may not want to tell you because of the shame. She will need to feel trust so that she can speak to you.

Some of the signs of sexual abuse in younger children include acting withdrawn, being anxious about everything, becoming extra clingy and not wanting to be left alone, and wetting the bed. They may start having nightmares or acting aggressively towards others. They may say sexual words or references that one would not expect a young child to know. Hearing a young child come out with such references can be very alarming, and this is a very good clue that sexual abuse is happening. Young children would not know of these things unless they are being subjected to something. Children also may not want to be in the company of certain people Please be vigilant with this, because this can also be a very good indicator that the person a child suddenly does not want to be around is the abuser. That fact can serve as a very big clue as to what is going on.

In older children, they may suddenly behave differently, like becoming withdrawn. They might begin to suffer from eating disorders like anorexia nervosa or bulimia, and they might act out by starting to play truant at school, missing classes. They might start exhibiting obsessive behaviour. They might start experimenting with drugs or alcohol. They may start to self-harm by cutting themselves, or they may have suicidal thoughts. They may exhibit anger towards you, other family members, or the world in general. They may also become sexually active or promiscuous.

If you see a sudden change in your child, it is your duty to find out what is going on. That child will feel so alone, as if she is the only person on the planet. She'll try to cope with the feelings that are over running through her young mind. What she is going through is too much for a little one to handle on her own. We need to notice problems and help our children before this goes on further and destroys their lives.

Sexual abuse can be a childhood destroyer, and it needs to be stopped dead in its tracks. The impact of abuse can last a lifetime if it is not disclosed or recognised. However, we must remember that every child and situation will be different.

The physical signs of abuse are soul destroying to a child, because it is unwanted, but the emotional and psychological effects left behind can cause more long-term harm. Self-blame is a big one. Victims feel they are to blame, and they are also manipulated or scared into believing they asked for it.

Later in life, as these children approach the teenage years and then grow into adulthood, some of them can have problems forming relationships. They may struggle with parenting their own children. They may have a problem with communicating with others, leading to anti-social behaviours. There is such a long list of negative emotional or psychological effects that can happen, and it makes me so sad to know that it often happens.

I am just one person, and I know that abuse or neglect will go on, but if I can save just one child from suffering, and if I can stop her from going through what I went through, it would make me so happy inside. We still have a long way to go, but educating others about what to look out for is a start.

Please,
help me !

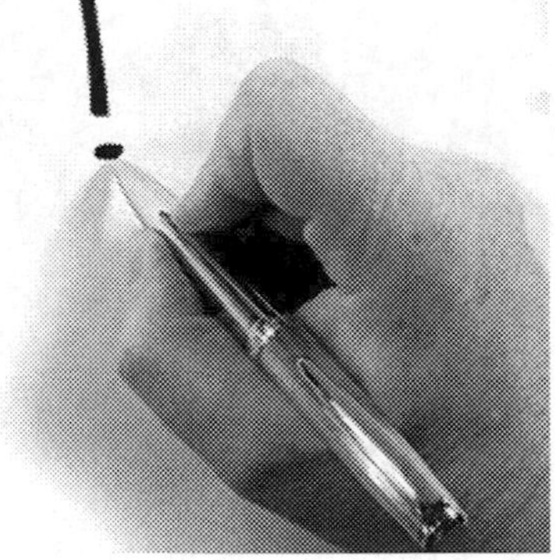

Appendix

Here is a list of organizations that can help victims, as well as people who want advice about something that doesn't feel right with regards to a child they feel is being abused or neglected.

The National Society of Prevention of Cruelty to Children. They are a service which runs twenty-four hours a day, seven days a week. Telephone them at 0808 800 5000. They have trained counsellors with whom you can speak. You may call them if you want advice about a matter concerning a child you suspect is suffering abuse.

Childline. Children can ring this service themselves if they want to tell someone what they are going through or what they may be feeling. They can be reached by telephone at 08001111. The calls are free and confidential, meaning that they what you say or discuss with them will not be told to anyone else if you don't want it to be. They are there to hear what you want to tell them, and there is no problem or issue too small or too big. Other children or young people who are going through the same problems as you will also use this service, and it is one to be used by children up to the age of nineteen. There is a message board service where you can be in touch with other children or young people who are going through similar issues. It can give you some support, and you can help to support others.

The Police. Telephone them at 999 or 101. They are an emergency service and are there to be of assistance if there is an emergency or a concern.

Social Services. This is another agency that can assist in the safety of children, though personally this would be the last route for me to take.

We adults have a duty of care to protect and keep our children safe from sexual abuse, harm, and danger. It is important to ensure that children feels like they can trust you, open up to you, and tell you about what they are feeling. It is also important that they don't feel like they are going to be in trouble for speaking up and speaking out.

The worst thing is to speak up and then not be believed. That is soul destroying and could push them over the edge. I have heard of stories where the child is not believed and then told that she is making it up! This is horrific to me. The thought of being told that must be terrifying, because all the child is looking for is a way out of the nightmare that is happening to her. This is her cry for help!

Any young child who cries for help and tells you that she is being sexually abused should be 100 per cent believed, especially the youngest ones, because they do not understand what has happened or is happening to them. This is not a subject to lie about when it comes out of the mouths of babes!

Children have no right to be exposed to sex before the time of consent. Their innocence is theirs till they choose to let it go. They should be sat down by their parents or guardians and shown that their private parts are private. No one has the right to touch or look at their private parts, and neither should they be asked to look or touch anyone else's. They need to be taught that no means no. They have the right to feel uncomfortable, and if anyone makes them feel uncomfortable, they must say no. It is their right to say it. Children should be told that if there is anything that upsets them, or if there is anything that is worrying them, they can talk to you. We should be making sure that our children understand that saying no to unwanted touching can be said even to a family member or to someone they love. They need to understand that they have control over their bodies and that their feelings should be respected. If children feel confident that they can say no to a family member, then they will more than likely be able to show the confidence to say no to someone that they do not know.

Abused children will have been told that the abuse is 'our little secret'. They need to be taught that there are good and bad secrets, and there is a difference between them. We need to teach children that the good secrets will make them feel good about themselves, but bad secrets will make them feel worried, sad, or frightened.

They need to be able to feel comfortable to speak up and out about any secret that makes them feel bad, and they have to be assured that telling a secret will not harm anybody in their family or someone that they love. This is one of the biggest threats that will be used by abusers, who are very clever at disguising their threats by using reverse psychology and manipulating their victims into not saying anything. Abusers use the feeling of fear that something bad will happen to loved ones if children say anything.

God knows that I have had my fair share of issues coming from being abused. But I want children to be enlightened to the dangers that are ever present in society. They need to know now. Let's help them to speak up and speak out!